Countdown to Navidad
A Family Christmas Across Borders

Karen White Porter

DEDICATION

This book is dedicated to Bob, Nancy,
Scott, Elaine, Mario, Mr. and Mrs.
Lopez, and the Guzman Family.

CONTENTS

ACKNOWLEDGMENTS

I am exceedingly grateful for the interesting adventures provided by Bob and Nancy, the information along the way from Scott and Elaine, the fantastic editing from Jim Porter, Helen and Chris Hooley, Pat Ashton, Grace Greenlie, Carol Ray Skipper, Elaine Beam Robinson, Ginny Dearinger, Barbara Bockman, and the inspiration from Wendy Dever who encouraged me to remember a Christmas of long ago, and most importantly the love and support from my daughter, and my dear husband.

1
CROSSING BORDERS
DECEMBER 14

I sat in the back seat of my Uncle Carl's brand new 73' Cadillac watching the wind shield wipers wipe away the sleet as Carl drove us to the airport. There was no chance we could turn back now. Half of me wanted to stay home and romp in the snow with Grandma. The other half of me was ready for adventure. I mostly worried about missing our normal Christmas traditions. This was the one time in my life I worried about Christmas. Would our visit to Mexico City the week before Christmas cause Santa to forget me? My father, mother, sister and brother knew how a Mexican Christmas worked from their days at the American Embassy in Mexico City. My brother Scott went there when he was one and lived there for four years. My sister Elaine was born there and left when she was two. At ten, I was the youngest and had never been there before. Mexico was all new to me. We turned and looked back at the cold drizzle on the Christmas lights on our block. Bob, my dad said, "We will be out of this drizzle and in the Mexican Sun soon."

If only there was a way, we could give Santa directions to the places we were visiting. I said nothing as we stood in line with our tickets and passports at the ticket counter. When we finally boarded the plane I was excited, because I got to sit by the window. First, we stopped in Atlanta for the international flight. Then we had to get our passports again and wait in line to go through customs on the American side to fly into Mexico. The wait seemed to take forever. I wondered why they fussed so much about going to another country.

My brother knew customs would take a while. When we finally landed in Mexico City, another long line awaited. The Mexican officials organized us with smiles and patience. We gave our yellow cards to the lady at the desk. Scott showed me how to fill out little yellow cards ahead of time. They explained that we weren't selling these presents for the Guzman family and the Lopez family to anyone. These cards were called customs declaration forms. My elder brother knew all about this because he had traveled to Mexico before, and was an avid reader. At 17 he was fully schooled in Latin culture, the complications of world travel, and the Spanish Language. He had even taken advanced Spanish.

Scott explained that the countries need to control what goes into the country in case a germ might hurt agriculture. They also wanted to be sure proper taxes were imposed on goods. All of these rules made the country safer. So, we had to get our bags and go through customs one more time. While we declared our belongings, I wondered if Santa had to go through this with all the presents he wanted to give children like me who lived in all the different countries around the world.

This customs process hadn't been quite as easy as we thought it would be. We would have to wait until the next day to begin our adventures, like going to a market, and visiting families our parents knew when they were living in Mexico. It was a busy airport and our parents hadn't been to Mexico for twelve years. Finding their way around took them longer than they had imagined it would. They rented a car. Then they headed for the Shirley Courts Motel. My dad did the driving, and he did his best, but he went the wrong way down one-way streets several times because they had changed the signs and street directions since he had been there last.

As I stepped onto the freshly mopped Mexican tile, my senses were awoken by the sound of the fountain, and the orange and brown and red and brown Mexican house finches chirping as they perched on the edge of the flower pots in the shade. This was a beautiful breezy paradise. My mother had planned for us to spend a while getting situated in the motel. The hanging festive red flowers, hanging piñatas, and cozy food counter made me wonder if Mom would let me wander off by myself into the gift shop or not. We met the cordial staff, and luckily my mom told us how to get around the hotel. This was her favorite place to stay in Mexico, because she had stayed here the first time she came to Mexico.

We went to bed early and woke up early for a day of shopping. My mother ordered the food for all of us from the menu the first morning. I didn't like hot spicy things. Even the eggs had chilis in them. It seemed everything came with beans, chilis and tortillas.

"But mom, I don't like tortillas for breakfast." I said.

My mother replied, "I will order you something simple like bananas" I liked that idea. "But, how do you say that?" I whined.

"*Platanos con leche*" Mom said. This meant bananas with milk. I needed a spoon, so she made hand motions to indicate a spoon. Say "*Cucharra, por favor.*" My mom taught me. I was quickly learning how to say the important things like this. She then gave me a few more important words "*con permiso.*" Which means excuse me. "*Por favor,*" which means please, and most important of all

"*Gracias!*" which means thank you. She said, "Thank you is the most important word." My head was all a buzz trying to remember this all. How could I ever learn to say "*platanos con leche por favor.*"? The man behind the counter smiled at me and talked to me in Spanish but I did not understand what he said. At least I knew he was nice because he smiled. Maybe I would learn how to say all this tomorrow. I quietly ate my bananas and milk. They were okay

Mom and Dad then took Scott, Elaine and me to the market. We each got forty pesos to buy whatever we wanted. Mom explained how to bargain.

"What does it mean to bargain?" I asked.

My mother replied, "First you say '¿*Cuanto questa*?' That means how much does it cost. Then, you act like you don't really want that object. Look at other things around it and ask how much they cost. Then once they tell you the price, you need to look surprised. Say '¿*Que*?' which means 'What?'. Then say '¡*No es vale la pena*!' which means 'It is not worth it.'. When they say '*Diez*' which means ten, you say '¿*Diez pesos*? ¡*Yo puedo pagar cinco*!' That means, 'I can pay five!' Then the shopkeeper will say '*No*' Then '*Nueve*' you say 'Five' and keep arguing until they might give in just a little bit. They might say "*Yo te lo regalo para ocho* (eight)!" which means I will give it to you as a gift for eight pesos. Then you smile and go a little down in price and say '*Siete*'(seven), in a sweet voice. They won't be able to turn you down."

I tried these tactics and I bought a woven straw purse, a doll hat that I later realized was made from already chewed chewing gum because it smelled like bad breath, and two marionette puppets. I had so much fun and it was soon time to go home and rest in the hotel to get ready for the next day. The next day was December 15. Only ten more days until Christmas Eve!

2
CULTURE SHOCK
DECEMBER 15

My first exotic restaurant experience in Mexico was not my first lapse into the imaginings of Christmas magic. For hours, and sometimes for days, I fell without realizing it into the private imaginary world of Christmas enchantment. I thought about Santa and how he magically came down the chimney and put presents in our stockings. I imagined the elves helping him gather the reindeer to set out on his journey from the north pole. But, then lately I was more puzzled by the whole production of Christmas my parents planned, as appealing as the complete belief was. Still Santa's love mesmerized me with the special feeling of generosity. Somehow, I knew love couldn't be broken apart. It is always there wherever you are, even in Mexico instead of Ohio. The Amazing expression of Christmas here gave me no reason to doubt Santa would find me. But, this restaurant Christmas experience almost awakened me from this dream.

After a long day of shopping at the market, we took a taxi back to the Shirley Courts Hotel. We made it there by three o'clock. It was quiet at the hotel, and all the daily cleaning and preparations for a beautiful stay were being finished. The maids were quietly mopping the clay tile floors. The gardener was watering the red geraniums in the courtyard. We had just enough time to get into the room, and get dressed up for dinner. I put on my pale blue dress with the Peter Pan collar. My dad had his orange vacation pants, and Elaine and Scott were wearing their bell bottom jeans. Elaine's jeans had patches all over them that she had sewn on by herself. These jeans always impressed me. My mom wore her red high-neck blouse with elegant ruffles and pearl buttons. Everyone was ready to go out to eat with the Guzman family.

Our whole family got dressed up for going out with the Guzmans. Before we went to the restaurant, we went to their house to visit for a while. Poinsettias lined the walkways. The Guzman's house was so welcoming. It was special there. When we got to the gate my brother stepped forward and rang the bell. The tall stone wall with broken glass on it encircled the house. Scott explained it was there to protect the house from thieves.

Maria and Jorge Guzman came to the door. They were the same couple my parents had known years before but with a few more grey hairs and a lot more children. Once we were through the gate, we saw mango, lemon and avocado trees all around the house. As we entered the front door the courtyard invited us in with fragrant flowers and beams of light shining in. I looked at the surrounding rooms and the gently closed doors as I stood in the center courtyard. I looked up and wanted to climb the staircase leading to more rooms upstairs. I thought it would be fun to have a bedroom that opened into a courtyard like that.

I hoped the other kids would let

me play hide and seek with them. The Guzman kids were running and playing, going in and out of doors, and up and down the stairs. They motioned for me to join them and my sister and I stayed together as a pair and joined them running everywhere in the house. We played hide and seek until the grownups were ready to go to dinner. We played together without words since my Spanish was not up to form. My dad and mom had worked in the American Embassy many years ago. The grownups spoke both English and Spanish. Señor Guzman and his family were old friends. They talked nostalgically about how much everyone had aged over the past ten years, and then yelled for all the children to come out from their hiding places and get in the car to go to the restaurant.

Señor Guzman had chosen a restaurant in downtown Mexico City called El Cardenal that was one of his family's favorite places to dine. He even invited his father-in-law, Pedro Mendez, to come and join us. Pedro was also a friend of our family. He used to babysit my brother Scott, and sister Elaine with the Guzman children on Friday evenings when they had gatherings at the embassy.

We all filed into the restaurant, and they had me sit next to Pedro because he was very good with children. He made funny animal shapes with the napkin that made me laugh and we were having a great time. My mom whispered in my ear and reminded me not to drink the water in the glass. It was important that I only drink the water from the bottle because I might get sick from drinking it. She explained that we Americans didn't have the same resistance to the germs in the water as the Mexican people who lived here and drank it every day.

My stomach rumbled, and I fidgeted from boredom. It seemed like the food was taking forever to get to the table. My mother ordered tamales. Scott ordered chilis relleno. Elaine ordered tacos. My dad ordered enchiladas. My mother told me to order a cheese quesadilla since it was not spicy. She also told the server in Spanish to not make it very spicy. They placed some guacamole and tortilla chips on the table in front of me. Grandpa Pedro showed me how to dip the chips in it. It tasted so good. Everyone else had some too. Soon the bowl had nothing left in it but crumbs. After that the food came, and I got my quesadilla.

The talking in the restaurant got louder and louder. All the grownups kept raising their voices to keep up with the conversation. I just kept quiet and thought about how odd it was to be here at Christmas. It just did not feel like Christmas with no snow, no Christmas lights, and no familiar English words or English Christmas songs on the radio. Then the waiter brought what I thought was a tray of salsa just for me to cheer me up. Grandpa Pedro winked at the waiter. This sauce must have been special. The green sauce the color of a light green Christmas tree, a red sauce as red as Santa's suit, and a yellow sauce as yellow as a shining Christmas star called the artist within me as if it were a pallet of paints.

I took my little spoon and decorated my quesadilla with the wonderful Christmas colors. A few eyebrows raised across the table, but no one said anything. My mother was talking with Mrs. Guzman about all the subjects their children were taking in school and comparing education systems. Grandpa Pedro was talking to my brother about the walks they used to take to Chapultepec Park when he had just learned to walk.

I took a huge bite out of my Christmas decoration. I was shocked and awed by the painful hot spicy spice. It was as if tiny green, yellow, and red hand grenades were ignited in my mouth. Water welled in my eyes and then poured down my cheeks. It burned and burned and burned. My tongue had never experienced this taste. My mouth was on fire. Messages were sent down my nerve endings that had never been sent before. At first, I tried to keep this experience to myself. After all we were in a public place. It hurt more with each swallow. I couldn't take it anymore. I let out a huge scream "AWWWWWWWWEEEEE" I took a drink of water. Then it got worse. My mom yelled "Leche por favor!!!"

I stopped crying once I took a sip of milk and everyone looked at me. They realized that I had used the extra hot spices reserved for Grandpa Pedro. Then they all started to laugh, and I began to cry out of embarrassment.

They tried to lift my spirits and reminded me there were only nine more days until Christmas Eve. "What do you think Santa will bring you? Or, are you going to wait for the day of the three kings for your presents?" Señor Guzman asked me. My mom said, "Santa is going to give some presents to the three Kings, and leave some in Ohio with Grandma." I could not think of presents, or Christmas at that moment. I just wanted the pain gone. My eyes didn't stop watering for over an hour.

3
A TRIP TO THE PYRAMIDS
DECEMBER 17

The next morning my parents let me sleep in. Everyone went to breakfast except my mom who was getting our water, sunscreen, sunglasses, hats, cameras, and snacks organized. When my dad, Scott, and Elaine came in and loudly said "Is she still asleep?" Her loud voice woke me up. My mouth was still burning from the night before. My lips were cracked from the peppers and the dry air.

Dad gave me a big hug and some Chapstick. He said, "How is my little chickadee today?"

I wrinkled my nose and said, "My beak is killing me from dipping into the hot sauce, big chickadee!" We laughed, Mom explained that it would help my mouth to eat something. I was afraid to eat ANYTHING at this point.

"Put on your comfortable walking shoes and your cotton smock shirt and come with me." My mom commanded. I quickly tied my comfortable cushy earth shoes and put my pink and white striped smock with pockets on. We went to the restaurant alongside the courtyard with the hanging red geraniums out front. Dad and my brother went to the concierge to arrange the day trip they had been planning. Before we got to the restaurant counter my mother repeated her Spanish lessons from the day before but tried to sweeten the experience a little for me today.

She directed me to sit and said, "Now say, '*Yo no quiero comida pecante.*' which means, I don't want any spicy food. This is how to order something that tastes better than anything you have ever eaten. say *'Por favor, yo quiero comer platanos con crema dulce.'* It sounded like this... (pour fa vor Yo kyiro komer platanoes kon krayma dool say).

I said what she told me to say, and then, Javier magically set a bowl, on a laced doily, filled with delicately sliced bananas with rich sweetened cream poured over them. I took a bite, and my tongue was soothed. The world was okay now. While I was eating, Mom explained that I could say this tomorrow and Javier, the waiter would give me the same thing. After I finished eating I kept practicing the words..."*Por favor, yo quiero comer platanos con crema dulce.*" "*Por favor, yo quiero comer platanos con crema dulce.*" "*Por favor, yo quiero comer platanos con crema.dulce*" "*Por favor, yo quiero comer platanos con crema dulce.*" "*Por favor, yo quiero comer platanos con crema dulce.*" I kept repeating it all morning in the car, on the trip, in the museum, up the stairs, and in the decorative gardens. "*Por favor, yo quiero comer platanos con crema dulce.*"

Mom said "*Nosotros tenemos cuarto (room)cuatro(four). Por favor cuando ella viene aqui en la mañana pondrá su desayuno en nuestro reciete.*" Javier smiled when it was explained that we were in room number four and that I could come in the morning to order breakfast, and that he should just put it on our room tab. He took pity on me when she went on to tell him what happened last night. He had a daughter my age who did not like spicy food either. After eating, it was time to join up with my dad, Elaine, and Scott. They had purchased tickets for seats in a large *van cooperativo* which is a van you can share with others and pay the driver together. This *cooperativo* left for the pyramids every day from the hotels. We all got in the van and sat down along with two other families.

I said, "Hey Scott, I can speak Spanish now. Listen to this! *'Por favor, yo quiero comer platanos con crema dulce.'*, *'Por favor, yo quiero comer platanos con crema dulce.'*, *'Por favor, yo quiero comer platanos con crema dulce.'* *'Por favor, yo quiero comer platanos con crema dulce.'*

My father sat up front with the

driver and explained in Spanish so I would not be embarassed"¡*Mi hija come un salsa de pimiento Savina Rojo ayer y no sabe que fue picante. Fue un sopresa grande!*" which meant, my daughter ate a huge Savina pepper yesterday for its beauty not knowing it would be hot. She got a huge surprise. They both laughed.

I kept practicing my Spanish. "*Yo no quiero comida picante.*" "*Yo no quiero comida picante.*" "*Yo no quiero comida picante.*" "*Por favor, yo quiero comer platanos con crema dulce.*" "*Por favor, yo quiero comer platanos con crema dulce.*" "*Por favor, yo quiero comer platanos con crema dulce.*" "*Por favor, yo quiero comer platanos con crema dulce.*" And they laughed even harder. I did not know it at the time, but he was explaining that I had eaten salsa of one of the hottest peppers that exist in the world. Apparently, there is a machismo attitude about anyone who can consume the hottest pepper. There is even a test they have in the Chile Pepper Institute at New Mexico State University. They measure the heat of the pepper. I had tried a pepper sauce that is now reported to score up to 577,000 on the Scoville scale. The Scoville chili testing scale is a measurement of the pungency (spicy heat) of chili peppers, or other spicy foods according to the website http://scovilleheatscale.com.

At last, I had recovered from my *picante* surprise and was ready to face the day. I looked out of the *cooperativo* window at the cobble stone streets and old buildings. The Spaniards had colonized this city, but many of the stones in the streets and the buildings had been taken from the indigenous people who had lived here and repurposed and rebuilt into the buildings we were now seeing. I did not realize the building material had been originally quarried by Aztecs until I saw the pyramids later that day.

There were roundabouts that we did not have back home. All the cars would go around in a circle to get to the turn they needed to turn into so people could get to where they were going. Many round-abouts had statues or fountains in the middle. There were so many monuments and statues of famous people who had lived in, fought for, and died for Mexico. All of this was on top of a great lake, which was on top of ruins of the old Aztec Empire, which was once a Mayan Empire. Mexico was a very old place.

As the driver took us down many busy streets with tall buildings. Then the buildings got shorter and the roads seemed less busy. The sun shined so brightly here. It was a different kind of light than I was used to in Ohio. A dry heat began to warm up the cobble stones beneath us. I was ready for an adventure. We got out of the van and walked up to the ticket booth. It was a stone and mortar shack with ticket windows. Signs were posted explaining the rules. No drinking, pets, or food. I could read the signs because they were in both Spanish and English. Since I was 10, my ticket was free. I was proud of that. Everyone else had to pay. This was just like a state park back home.

The barren dry scenery here was quite different from the slushy cold snow in Ohio. There were mountains in the distance. The sky was a stark blue. The land was almost like a desert. There were agave plants with long spikey pointy leaves shrubs, and cacti everywhere. The trees had a gnarly dry look to them as if they were bent over and struggling just to survive in this parched earth. The plants here had a way of surviving in this dry place by taking in the most water they could and saving water within their stems when it did rain. The altitude was at 7482 feet above sea level. We put on our sunscreen and hats and were each given our water bottle. We had to protect ourselves because the air was thinner here at this altitude. The UV rays could more easily come in contact with our pale Ohio winter skin. Each of us were told to make our water last, because there would be no more water until we came back.

The pathway to the pyramid was lined with stones on both sides led the way to the main pyramid of the sun. It did not look like it was too far, but that was deceiving. When we arrived at the foot of the Pyramid of the Sun the inclines were not steep. So, walking up a level took time because the slope was gradual. It was at a slight gradient. When we got to the top of that level, we would see the next level. I'd think it was the second to last level, but still there seemed to be another level, and another and another. I began to get tired. My brother kept cheering me on. "You can do it!" I was even getting flushed from the sun. My feet were dragging. We were determined to get to the top. The map said there were two main pyramids. The *Pyramid of the Sun* and the *Pyramid of the Moon*. We wanted to do both. The climb was exhausting. My brother explained to me that this complex of pyramids was built in 100 BC. The Toltecs believed their Goddess Ichpochtli would provide sustenance and rain for them. Then they had drought and not enough rain to sustain them. The city could not provide for so many people and they left. The city was in ruins when the Aztecs took over hundreds of years later. I thought to myself, here we were at Christmastime celebrating the birth of Jesus, and this place was built one hundred years before he was born, for a Goddess.

It was all one big project. There were so many interesting decks. It was called the *Pyramid of the Sun* by the Aztecs. The Aztecs believed Chocmool would rest here and be an intermediary for the Aztec sun god Huitzilopochtli's ancient ceremonies with human sacrifices. The priests who ripped the hearts out of their sacrificial victims, believed the sun was set in motion by Huitzilopochtli to set time in motion. For this reason, they monitored and recorded the placement of the stars and the moon in the sky, which were Huitzilopochtli's brothers and sisters which he was chasing to protect his

mother.   This pyramid was massive.
We kept climbing.   The steps kept
getting steeper and steeper to the point
where I grabbed on to the step-in front
of myself to pull my body up.

When I got to the in-between
level, I had to stop to catch my breath.
When I stopped and looked down, it
looked sooo steep. When I looked
around, I got a sense of the vastness of
this place.   You could see for miles
around. Looking down on the ruins
you could see outlines of different
buildings on the road leading up to this
main pyramid.   At one time 200,000
people had lived here. That was ten
times the size of Worthington, the
suburb of Columbus where we lived.
People lived, died, worshiped, played
games, shopped, farmed, ate, and

learned here.

My brother told me there was a Coke machine at the top and so I got a new burst of energy. We climbed and climbed, and soon we made it to the top. Alas, there was no Coke machine at the top. He had been joking. I was not mad, because the view was worth it. I had my Brownie camera, so I took pictures all around. We saw the temple of the Jaguar and the Pyramid of the moon. The Temple of Quetzalcotal. Off to the side near *'Avenida de los Muertos'* (Street of the Dead) a group of people inside a fence were bent over buckets and dirt and mounds of dirt. They almost looked like ants we were so high up.

"What are they doing down there? "I said.

"They are digging to see if they can see artifacts like the ones we will see in the museum," my brother replied,

"What are artifacts?" I asked.

"They are things people made a long time ago that got buried in the earth, that will tell us about the time those people lived in. Can you imagine what this place would have looked like when people lived here so long ago?" Scott said. I thought for some time about that. After a short rest, it was time to go back down the pyramid again. We went down to ground level and found we could go down even farther. There was a hidden tunnel that allowed a priest to suddenly appear up top. I wondered if that tunnel was a secret passageway so many centuries ago as I walked down the stairs into the cool dark tunnel. It was really dark underneath the *Pyramid of the Sun.* Luckily there were hand rails to hold onto. We investigated a blocked off passageway next to the tunnel we were in linking us to the area where the food and souvenir stands were. Down, down, down, below through a narrow cave like walkway we could see inside where the priests met to start a ceremony. Paintings of dragons and different leaves and Aztec lettering on the walls told us something we could not read, and no translations have been made so far. The dragon gargoyles looked almost Chinese. The carved pillars with representations of the Gods worshipped by the Toltecs, and then later the Aztecs were a mystery to me. They still had a history here. I did not know where to start asking questions. Something so different from my life experience left me speechless. The painted frescos of the feathered serpent with a beak and scales zig zagged on the walls as it swallowed the tail of the next serpent and so on. That was the Toltec Goddess of rain. They must have been painted deeply into the wall for me to be able to see them over a thousand years later. There were bits of paintings on the walls that could no longer be seen due to the weathering action over time. The tunnel emerged out into a ballcourt. They believe there was a game played here. There were gargoyles on the walls with holes in them perhaps for a ball to go through.

It was truly a sight to see. What was the meaning of all this? My dad told me they still do not entirely know.

And when I came out from the depths below, into the ballcourt the light shined on me and I saw the stalls selling trinkets for tourists. I had quickly ascended from the ancient mysterious priests' tunnel. We were told that there was a passageway to an upper level they might have used to sneak up to their pulpit to surprise their believers below them as magically appeared. It was by no magic that our tunnel took us to venders ready for visitors. The park service was keen on making a little extra money. This shop would raise more funds for their digs. I looked at what they had to sell. I bought a red dragon whistle made from clay. I could blow through it and make music.

We headed up the steps to meet mom and dad for lunch at the ground level. I felt hot and had to go to the bathroom. Surprisingly this was the coolest time of year here. We thought we could get a cool place to eat with bathrooms because not many people came here at Christmas time. But we found out, we had to go to the public bathroom for all tourists before we ate because the restaurant had no bathrooms. A big crowd stood in a long line and a short old lady with long black braided hair, and a very worn face wearing a blanket over her dress to keep warm stood by the line to the woman's room holding a basket of pieces of old newspaper. My brother said the blanket was a *sarape.* I had never seen someone wearing a blanket like that. It had Mexican designs in it like the ones in the market and narrower like a shawl. It was hand woven with faded colors and more fringed at the ends than most sarapes. When we got closer to the front of the line we found out, the old lady with the *sarape* was selling pieces of newsprint for 5 centavos a piece as makeshift toilet paper. My mom explained that was a way to recycle newspaper and save money on toilet paper as well as a way for a poor old lady to make a living. I wanted to get out of that hot stinky area, but I had to go. So, I quickly paid for my paper, and used it as it was intended to be used. It worked, but was a lot more rough than any toilet paper I had ever used. It was weird putting used toilet paper in a garbage can rather than flushing it. But alas the plumbing could not contain the paper. After we used the bathroom we walked over to the fence.

I had seen this area from above. This is where the archeologists were digging. I grabbed the chain link fence and leaned against it. I was so tired from the climb.

"What are they digging for?" I asked my mom..

"They are looking for things in the dirt like bones or pottery or stuff like that", Mom said.

"Why do they have a fence around it?" I asked.

"So other people don't go in." She said. Some square sections were cordoned off with string. People were gathering the dirt and sifting through it. Each little rock was being checked and brushed with a special brush.

Mom said they would date and categorize each piece and record it in a book. Mom and I walked to a sign about this dig. The sign said some artifacts dated back to 100 BC. It was hard to imagine that this place was built around the time Jesus was born. I was told that the north star aligned perfectly with the tallest mountain that can be seen from this valley on four days before Christmas day every year. I wondered if the people who lived here at that time knew the special importance of that star. I was glad the people here now mostly believed in Jesus and didn't make human sacrifices any more. On the drive back to the hotel, I wondered what it must have been like in that old city when people lived there so long ago. I blew my clay whistle until my parents got irritated and then told me to stop. Then I fell into a deep sleep listening to the hum of the engine, and soon we were back at the hotel ready for a light *'cena.'* *'Cena'* is the Spanish word for supper. Tomorrow it would be only eight more days until Navidad, the celebration at midnight when Jesus was born.

4
MEXICAN CARTOONS
DECEMBER 18

After that big day at Chapultepec

the muscles in my legs quivered, and my nose was sun burned. As soon as my head hit the pillow, I began to dream of steps. For those of us who did not fall asleep right away, we had books to quietly read. I drifted off only to be awoken by a clattering around in the bathroom at about 3:00 am, and my brother's voice outside the bathroom door

"Hurry Up!!! I can't wait." He said.

Then the voice from within the toilet. "I will be as quick as I can," My mom replied. It was like changing of the guards. After a while my mom said "I feel better. I will go ask the maid for extra toilet paper. There is Pepto Bismol, and Imodium D in my suitcase." Everyone had a spoonful or two of Pepto Bismol, except for me. I think I owed my iron stomach, and lack of diarrhea to my trusty dusty phrase *'Por favor, yo quiero platanos con crema dulce.'*

That morning everyone stayed in the hotel rooms going to the bathroom and resting while I began my early morning routine. I woke at my usual 6:00 am and quickly got dressed. After I brushed my teeth, I went to the restaurant. No one was there but me. I sat on the red stool, under the serving counter and said my charming phrase when Señor Javier came around "*Yo quiero platanos con crema dulce por favor. No quiero comida picante.*" Again, Javier provided his special banana bowl just the way I liked it. I was empowered. I savored my bananas and day dreamed of presents I would get for Christmas that year. I went back to the room to watch more cartoons for the rest of the day.

My mom warned us before we left on our trip that travelers often get diarrhea from eating and drinking foods and beverages that the people who live there eat every day. That is why she had packed Pepto Bismol. That is why we weren't allowed to buy popsicles that the street vendors sold. My mom wanted to trace where the germs came from that got them sick. Was it that last meal? Scott thought he had immunity from his stay in Mexico because he lived there with a family for six months and had constant, repeated exposure to the germs that we were just experiencing. He did not think he could still get sick again, but he did!

My parents even remembered that when they first came to Mexico they got a bit of a tummy bug that went away, and then after that they could handle more foods. They knew however, that the plumbing system just couldn't handle the huge population, and the earthquakes over time disabled the plumbing system so sewage could leak into water pipes. Some people kept their immunity they got in Mexico, while other people found that they would have to get used to everything all over again when they came back. Bob and Nancy did not want to take any more chances.

My dad said, "I guess we all have Montezuma's revenge." I then replied "Speak for yourself, big Chickadee! By the way, what is Montezuma's revenge?" He laughed and went on to explain that Montezuma II was Emperor of Mexico in the 1500's when the Spanish took the Aztec Empire.

The story goes that he had to get back at the conquerors somehow for taking over Aztec land and people. These diarrhea germs were his way of retribution. Being colonized was hard on the native people. If all this land was Montezuma's at one point, I can see why he might have reason to make foreigners pay for the hardships they had once caused him. But, I was not especially mad at Montezuma. I was thankful for a day of rest. I was tired and worn out from so much walking.

Elaine, Scott, and I got as much orange pop as we wanted, and I got to watch Mexican cartoons. It was hilarious to hear Bugs Bunny with a deep voice speaking Spanish. I kept watching reruns of Superman. My brother kept telling me the Spanish translation of "It's a bird!, It's a plane!, no! It's Superman! Hearing *"¡Es un pajaro!, ¡Es un avion!, ¡No. Es Superhombre!!"* repeatedly drilled the words into my memory forever.

My brother translated the children's cartoon *"Los Tres Reyes Magos"* from Spanish to English for me. This cartoon can still be seen on YouTube today at. https://www.youtube.com/watch?v=Frt7nki0fqI.

It was the story of Jesus' birth, Angel Gabriel, and the Three Kings. I realized then that the Three Kings were important here. The funny part about the film was that Mary was dressed in Mexican clothes, and the village looked like a Mexican village. There were cacti, and burros, and everything in the film was as if the story of Jesus had taken place in Mexico. My family sat in the hotel room drinking hot tea and eating saltine crackers until everyone was better. Only I had the stomach for the orange soda pop.

5
EL BALLET FOLKLORIKO
DECEMBER 19

The next day everyone was feeling better. I was still the first awake, dressed, and out of the room. The family met me at the breakfast counter in the hotel. I was eating my '*platanos con crema.*' Javier had taught me a new phrase '*te caliente con limón.*' I loved hot tea with lemon. Everyone ate breakfast together and we decided to go to see the ballet today. I loved the ballet too. Our family went to see the Nutcracker every Christmas. I wonder if they would have Christmas ballet. So, we got tickets to see *El Baile Folkórico.* That translated to "folk dance." I imagined head scarfs, long skirts and a lot of stuff like square dancing we did in the gym at school. I had hoped it would be a little bit more than that. It probably was going to be a bit more sparkly. After all it was going to be at the *'Palacio de Bellas Artes'(*Palace of the Beautiful Arts*)*.

It was a palace for arts. This palace had long curved marble staircases that swept elegantly upward. The geometrically styled art, paintings, metal work, and gold inlay focused on themes of the indigenous people and Spanish history. It blended together to create a classy culturally rich royal feeling. The precise and boldly delineated geometric shapes and strong colors impressed me. I felt important when I walked up the clean white and black checkered polished steps. The dragon scale roof tiles and native art reminded me of the pyramids. Yet here the Azteca symbolism showed Mexico's culture off but in present day form. I walked up the steps to the theater and grabbed onto the gold railings as my mother held my hand to make sure I did not get lost in the crowd.

This mix of cultures and ideas was in the very tile I walked on. My patent leather shoes made a special clicking sound on the marble steps and the black and white inlaid tile on the upper level was so shiny. We had seats in the middle of the orchestra area. When we sat down on the second level I looked to both sides and saw three levels of box seats where there were people in them already. We looked toward the big stage, and watched in anticipation for the dances of Mexico.

The curtain rose and soon ladies entered with huge skirts. They could wave these in the air like flowers dancing in the wind to music. The men then entered clicking their heals on the floor and raised their arms as they clicked their castanets. As the men and women paired off they stared into each other's eyes as if in a trance.

Dance after dance represented the people and their history. Some dances were of war and revolution. Some dances were of family and love. Some dances were of hospitality and agriculture. As I sat in the posh chair dressed up in my white dress and shiny shoes, I imagined myself learning to use the castanets too. I was soaking in the radiance and joy of this beautiful place.

Baile Folklórico, literally means "folk dance" as translated to English, also known as ballet folklórico, are **Indigenous** dances from the different parts of Mexico. There were 12 dances in the program that night. Each one had a story of a region or a history of Mexico. Each group had a different costume. Women dancing with machine guns surprised me with their strength that told the story of how they fought alongside the men during the war of independence. Their big skirts swished up and down as they raised machine guns in the air. They twirled and made huge colorful circles on the stage.

The men wore black pants with **tassels** on each side of the leg, a red tie and belt and a black wide-brimmed hat. Some women had tighter fitting and shorter skirts and either white or black boots. Other women had brightly colored ruffled skirts trimmed with ribbons with heels that clanked loudly when they danced. Their fancy hair had elaborately styled hair with carved bone fans in them. Some women had lacey white dresses.

A Mariachi band played for the dancers. At the end the Guitaristas, Vihuelistas, Vihuelasitas (The vihuela is a creation of the Coca Indians of Southwestern Jalisco in Mexico.), Guitarrons, and trumpet players came out. The audience applauded when the dancers bowed to them. At the end of the program I was amazed at the stained-glass curtain that came down at the end of the show. It took my breath away. Angels and Greek looking gods and goddesses with grapes adorned the outside. But the Gods and goddesses were Aztec. Pillars like the ones they must have had in the Parthenon were on the outside. I barely had time to take in all these murals painted on all the walls, but they were grand. The Palace impressed me, but the dances impressed me even more. Now it was time to go home and rest up for our trip to El Salvador where we would meet up with Mario and his family.

6
THE HOUSE IN THE MOUNTAINS
DECEMBER 20

The next day we got up early and went to the airport to fly to El Salvador. Again, we had to go through customs with the Mexican officials and explain to them we were not taking anything but gifts to El Salvador. Then we had to go through customs with the El Salvadorian officials to make sure we were not bringing anything troublesome into the country. Each time we had to show our passport. Each time they looked through our bags to make sure we were telling the truth. I learned a lot about borders. I hoped Santa Claus would be able to cross the border and bring gifts to the children. I wondered if the people here had to depend on the Three Kings for their presents because they could pass through borders without having to go through customs like we did. Santa on the other hand would have to go through customs because he could be detected by radar and brought down by security. The Three Kings traveled through dry arid dessert like land with camels at night.

This cross-cultural exchange fun was stressful for me at Christmastime, because I didn't know what was going to happen next. At least I could count on Mario our former El Salvadorian exchange student to pick us up at the airport with his dad. I learned to love Mario like a brother when he lived at our house and went everywhere with my brother Scott. I was so excited because he was going to take us to see the volcano. Then he was going to help us navigate to San Salvador from

Mexico. So, we got on a plane and went to the city of San Salvador in the country of El Salvador to meet Mario at the airport. Mario's father had a house in the mountains, a house in the city, and a house at the beach. They had plans to take us to all three of these houses before Christmas. So, in the morning Mario, and his dad woke us up early and said

"Today we are going to see Ilamatepec."

I said "What? Did you say, 'lame tape'?"

They replied "No it is pronounced "ya ma tay pec"

I had never seen a volcano, so I was excited. It was 70 miles west of San Salvador city. When we left the city, we were going up into the craggy mountains. We stopped to shop at a store that sold my favorite delicacies: a pastry shop! The pastries were huge, sweet and flakey. We got in the rental car. Señor Lopez, Mario's dad, drove, and drove, and drove. The mountains were getting closer and closer. We were going higher and higher. The roads were more and more twisty turns, and windy twists, they went this way and that way and soon we were at a desolate national park with a few small signs.

We had our water bottles, snacks, and good walking shoes. We were ready to visit and climb the path to the top. The coffee bean trees were set along the paths and you could see the beans being dried in the sun to ripen just right. This was the place coffee was grown. The sign at the front of the entrance read "Cerro Verde National Park." They were proud of this park. I guess it was a special landmark.

Mario took a 10-*colón* bank note out of his pocket. On it you could see the volcano. I looked up and could see a slight bit of smoke or steam coming out of the tippy top of the volcano. I wondered if we would see lava here. I worried about whether we were safe. They told me not to worry, because there is occasionally a bit of lava that comes out of the top. No one ever gets hurt by it because no one can get that close to it.

After our hike, we came back down the mountain and drove up another mountain to a hotel on the nearby Cerro Verde. The terrace supported us as we looked from it to view the erupting volcano. I felt queasy, nauseous, and dizzy. My mom said this was altitude sickness. We were not as high up in altitude on Cerro Verde. There seemed to be more air around, in just a ten-minute drive from the top of the other mountain. I felt a bit less queasy. My mom thought it would be a good idea to have a light evening meal.

When we arrived at the guest house near the volcano, A big sign that said *"Pupusería"* listed the prices and delectable treats we could have if we were hungry or thirsty. I of course wanted them all right then. My mother insisted I wait for dinner. She wanted me to learn how the native people cooked their pupusas. *Pupusas* are an El Salvador favorite. They are made with *masa* from corn. *Masa* is basically a corn dough. Corn is a main element in most people's cooking there. The process of making these *pupusas* has been around for a long time.

First Maria showed us a basket of dried corn. She took each dry ear of corn and pulled the kernels out with a prong. Then she showed us the big pot where she quickly boiled the kernels with lime powder to soften the skin of the kernel. The corn was now wet but still al dente. She then took a spoonful of the corn and put it in the stone mortar. She held the pestle and ground the boiled kernels.

Once she ground it down to a dough-like consistency, she took a tablespoon of the coarse *masa* dough and rolled it into a ball. She added a bit of water to re-grind it into a finer dough.

Then she flattened out a patty and put cheese and sausage and onions in the middle of it and folded it over. Then she flattened it out once more. Now it was flat corn dough with a tasty surprise inside. There was a huge griddle on an open fire in a limestone fire pit. The hot coals slowly cooked the *pupusos* perfectly browned on the outside with perfectly melted cheese and onions on the inside. An ooey gooey luscious dribble of cheese dangled out of my first bite as if popping out from a game of hide and seek.We ate these on the tile veranda overlooking the mountains. The glow of the volcano enchanted me.

Scott showed me the stamp Mario had sent him a long time ago for his stamp collection that he kept in his wallet. The volcano on the stamp said, "*El Faro del Pacífico*" which meant "The Lighthouse of the Pacific." Now we got to see this volcano in real life, and it wasn't just a stamp from the mail any more. When the sun set, a beautiful orange sky had just left and turned to black.

Once night fell, it got dark outside. The stars shined more brightly than I had ever seen because there were no lights on for miles around. The darkness of the night was unforgettably stark. We sat on the veranda in the cool mountain night air. We could see the glow of the lava in the distance as we ate our evening meal by candle light. Now I knew why it was called 'Lighthouse of the Pacific'. Then the glow of the lava in the distance glowed an orangey red color. The cool air surrounded me, and I began to feel a chill. I was grateful I had brought a sweater. I fell asleep on the way home with my head resting on the shoulder of my older exchange student brother, Mario, in the back seat. It had truly been an adventurous day. The next day was December 21. Only three more days until Christmas eve, when I could stay up until Christmas day! I had never done that before.

7
LA PLAYA
DECEMBER 21

I awoke late that night from the long car ride when the engine's humming stopped. We had arrived at the beach house. Mr. Lopez had a family living there who was looking after the place. We met up with them and it was a grand home made from metal. It included a tall ceiling and huge tin roofs. We were quickly shown our bedrooms, so we could get a good night's sleep for our beach trip the next day. There were huge windows, and you could hear the waves of the ocean from where we slept. The house we stayed in was made of tin. When it rained, the '*tap tap tap*' of the droplets was like percussion instruments keeping a strange beat as the frogs and birds chirped. As you slept in the early morning heard rustling around by the lady of the house as she made us El Salvadorian pupusas. You could hear the old abuela grinding the corn in the stone grinders. The delicious smell of the pupusas frying on an outdoor open fire wafted into my bedroom. My stomach started to growl.

I was still in that morning waking time just lying there filling my senses with all the sounds and smells of this new place. Soon, I felt my mother's cold hands on my face, gently waking me up enough to open my eyes. It was time to go to the shrimp boat. I put on my bathing suit and shirt. When I looked out the window, I saw coconut trees were all around. One of the young boys climbed up to the top of the tree to get me a coconut for us to eat. He put a hole in the coconut and let me drink it before we left for the boat. The coconut milk was tangy and fresh. I still seemed tired, and so they gave me coffee too. The coffee here was for kids too. It was delicious with lots of milk. After the coffee I was ready to go!

We got a bucket full of magazines and soda pop and we took the motorboat out to sea. Soon we saw a shrimp boat. We hoisted the treats up to the sailors. They, in turn, hoisted a bucket full of shrimp down to us. They would be on the boat until they caught their quota, which could be days from now. This trade was great for all of us. When we got home, Señora Lopez made shrimp with cream sauce over rice. She served it for dinner that night.

The next day we went swimming

at the beach and ate cold shrimp sandwiches for lunch. All the big kids went shark hunting with Mr. Lopez. I tasted *jugo* de tamarind (tamarind juice), and *jugo* de guava (guava juice) for the first time. I played in the sand with Mario's little sister. I looked at the white sand and tried not to think of snow and sledding down the big hill at Antrim Park in Worthington.

"Let's make angels in the sand!" I asked Mario to translate what I was doing. I laid down and moved my hands and feet across the white beach sand. I stood up and pointed to the impression it had made.

Margarita looked at it and giggled. "Un angelita! Claro!" Then she did the same.

Here it was only four days till

Christmas and we were making sand angels everywhere up and down the beach. We kept making them until there were angels everywhere up and down the beach. We laughed together because we had a new game to play.

"Bonita Chiquita Margarita," Mario said. This means pretty little Margarita. In Spanish, when you call something small it is a term of endearment in Spanish.We laughed and danced and made sand castles after that. Then, we ran into the ocean to wash the sand off ourselves only to come back to the beach to take turns burying each other in the sand. After that we ran along the shore collecting shells. The sun warmed our backs. We wanted to stay outside forever, but our parents knew better. So, we had to come back to eat our main meal of they called (*almuerzo*), We sipped the soup and slowly savored shrimp with rice and beans along with ayote, (a tropical squash) around two or three O'clock.

I was so full and ready to nap in the heat of the day. Margarita lay in the bed next to me. The gift of her friendship would be treasured throughout my life. Sharing this moment was worth more than any souvenir I could take home. We napped on cool white sheets with a hand crocheted afghan over us. The peaceful breeze calmed me. The crashing of the waves against the shore lulled us to sleep. Margarita fell asleep first. It was odd, but she slept with her eyes open. I tried not to sleep, but when it started to rain, and the pitter patter pit pit pat of the rain on the tin roof hypnotically sounded, I could not keep my eyes from feeling heavy and finally closing. I was again awakened by the grinding of the corn along with the pitter patter of the rain and the smell of the puposas and arepas cooking on the outdoor stove.

The parents had taken their siesta too. Everyone enjoyed each other's company. Later on, the evening meal was called 'cena,' and it was not a huge portion of food. But everyone had a light coffee and began to talk until way after the sun set, and millions of stars were out. Then Señor Lopez insisted we walk along the beach. An El Salvadorian sunset was unlike any other, he said. When we got to the beach we realized he was right. The reflection on the calm gulf waters of the blazing orange sun and the pale blue sky spread across the water and seemed to look as if it had been dotted by whipped-cream clouds. It reminded me of the sherbet orange Push-Ups I ate in school. The tangerine colored sky was powerfully orange. You could almost taste the orange with your eyes.

8

REGALOS
DECEMBER 22

The peace of the tropical sunset had deserted the zocalo, or town center. Shouting vendors had descended upon the Mercado Central nearby and people unfurled their loads on the ground some had carried for miles. Other vendors and little tents had set up kitchens. We had already shopped in the Mexican Markets; but the Salvadorian markets were different. The spaces were smaller and more energetic. More lives depended on making a sale. The people were more personal and looked in your eyes more deeply. The market had everything, it seemed. The people brushed against you as you passed by. I felt the energy of this throng, and my mother insisted on holding my hand, so I would not get lost. In some places you could not see above the crowd and you could easily get lost. Colorful blankets spread out before us had everything on them.

Food cooked on stoves this morning displayed next to jewelry, bracelets, and necklaces woven or beaded by a grandmother in the mountains. Onions, radishes, cilantro garlic with their leaves still on them were ready to be purchased, chopped and put into a stew at home. Parents, children, and friends ran yelling about what was the most important item to buy. Nuts, watermelon seeds, dried fruit, and amaranth had been hand-dried in the sun on a cool mountain ledge. They probably had been gathered and saved these for weeks for this special sale day. "Grapes, or chilis?" More yelling ensued because they could not decide. Cabbages, sat next to carts of shirts with weavings and nylon umbrellas. A vendor argued with a man bargaining the price of her pupusas she cooked on a grill. "Diez colones sin salsa" "No, con salsa!", She kept on cooking while bargaining. Her sister was in the next stall selling clothes, cheese she had made from the goats she milked, and pastries her mother in law made, along with pottery she had hand painted. The different painted plates had beautiful roosters, and rabbits painted on them. The, silver jewelry was fine and detailed. The next stall had some chickens that looked tired and worn out from being tied up side down on a stick that had been carried for miles. The chicken that was freshly slaughtered looked a lot like the kind you could buy at the grocery store at home. The freshly caught fish reminded me of the fishing village we had visited. I wondered if people from the village would sell their fish to buy crates of dried corn that sat around the corner. They could feed more people with that. The crates of onions smelled earthy. The people sitting on crates looked tired. The little wrapped bits they called 'dulces', were candy of all different colors shapes and sizes that looked like something I would want to try, but my mother pulled me away.

The towels and posters of Pele the famous soccer player swung back and forth, next to the umbrellas hanging up high but people's heads brushed against them. The intensity of the people weighing their goods amazed me. The hanging signs mystified me because I did not understand what exactly it was they were trying to say. The papayas, balloons and watermelons could be bought from the women in aprons cooking next to the pañatas for sale but if you wanted to buy the spices like achiote, and mixed herbs too, you had to pay the woman with the woven and embroidered purse. She was nice and took time to explain to my mom how different spices were for different things. There were spices to put in the milk for children to help them sleep, spices to cook your chicken with and so on. Mario said we really should try buying the shoes made from tires because they lasted a long time. But I could not decide, because the same vendor had shoes made from wood, straw, leather, and fabric. The assortment and odd styles confounded me. Besides, the shirts, skirts, bags, and pants were interesting to look at too. I felt lost in this sea of things.

My mother told me today was my chance to buy presents for the poor people in the village where we were going tomorrow. She explained that Jesus taught us that it is better to give than it is to receive. And that we should not be focusing on presents this Christmas, because the trip itself was our Christmas present.

"What would a little girl my age want?" I asked Señor Lopez.

"Shoes." He said quietly with a

serious look on his face. He had been one of these poor children once. He made his way up to be an important business man here by selling combs in the street. He knew what it was like to be without shoes. And so, we bought shoes of all shapes sizes and types.

After cena (dinner), we went to bed early. I drifted off thinking about the presents we were giving the village. I wondered why we did not wrap them. In just two days we would be celebrating Christmas eve. In just two days I could stay up till midnight. My parents never let me stay up late on Christmas eve before.

9
A POOR FISHING VILLIAGE
DECEMBER 23

We got up at six. I got dressed. I brushed my teeth and asked Señora Lopez for my usual favorite breakfast. *"Por favor, yo quiero platanos con crema. Yo no quiero comida picante."* She made that for me and had pitchers of juice on the table along with some pastries too. I tried everything. We all sat around the table and ate together. Mario pointed up at the chandelier. It was moving.

"This is a mini earthquake. We call it a temblor which is a tremor in English. We have them all the time. Isn't that cool?" We were all impressed. I had just experienced my first tremor. The realization that the ground beneath our feet is not as solid as we think made me stop and think that life was not as certain as I thought.

Another realization about gifts and those who had little to give, was about to change me. Today we were going to a poor fishing village. We grabbed our bottled water and got into the van. Mario's father explained that this place was too far away from the beach house or for any one there to get to work in the city without a car. "This trip is *'vale la pena'*, which means (worth it.)" he said. "This is where Señora Lopez and I received one of the biggest presents of our life." As he said this, his eyes misted over. The rainy season provided fish in the rivers they could sell at market, but at times the rainy season did not come. That is when the villagers went hungry. I wondered how a place so poor could provide any kind of present?

We drove into the *"bosque"* (woods). I loved being among the trees. I used to love walking under the massive shade of their leaves behind my house in Worthington. But, these woods were different. They went on and on and did not seem to have the same lush shade. It was as if they had been picked clean of anything that could provide the birds and critters with food. This was because the people had taken what they could to provide wood for their stoves.

The tarmac road turned into a dirt road. So, we followed the ruts in the grass along a river for a while. Then we went up a hill where we saw the village. It was unlike any community of people I had ever seen.

The houses were not made of bricks, stucco, or wood. They were made of pallets, cardboard boxes, and jagged used tin-siding like the pieces left in the rubbish pile out by the far barn at Uncle Bucks farm in Ohio. There were a lot of children running around. They were dirty and did not have shoes.

An old grandmother, Señor Lopez, called '*Abuela*', was standing by a smoky wood stove making tortillas. She lived in one of the traditional huts made from palm fronds. She offered us food, but Mario's father had warned us in the car that we should decline any offers of food for two reasons. First, the villagers did not have enough food to feed themselves, and second, there was no proper sanitation there, and it might make us sick. He told us to tell them that we had eaten a big breakfast and were not hungry. The stove was a rickety temporary black piece of steel that had a big, heavy griddle. It looked as if everyone cooked there. There was a mortar and pestle for grinding the dry corn. On the floor of the hut there was a bucket full of river water and lye to soak the corn for softening. Abuela ground the soaked hominy grits just like the grits at the beach house, but she used a rusty grinder to make her tortillas. Sometimes children did not have food. They got fed last because their papa needed the energy to work. That is why the children were so thin. Holes in their roofs let rain in. There was enough to eat when they had money to buy corn. The dirt floors did not protect their bare feet from the worms in the sand. The walls of the kitchen were made from palm fronds. The sleeping quarters were made from discarded materials. There was an outdoor toilet I did not want to use. The drinking water from the river was not safe to drink, but they had to drink it anyway. The family could be evicted at any time because this land did not belong to them.

"Why?" I asked Señor Lopez.

"Because they are poor," He said.

"Why?" I asked.

"Because they have no education and cannot get a job."

"Why?" I asked.

"Because they live too far away from the city."

"Why can't they move?"

"Because they have no money."

I then realized that if I were going to ask why again it would take me back to my first question. Now I truly knew what a vicious circle it was. It seemed brutal and unfair. I wondered if it could ever be changed.

We toured the village. The *Abuela* smiled at me and gave me a flower for my hair. Señor Lopez explained that I had never seen how to make pupusas. My mother whispered in my ear that I should pretend that I had not yet seen pupusa making. *Abuela* showed me how she made pupusas. She gathered a small handful of masa between the palms of her wet hands with pride just as her mother, and grandmother, and great grandmother before that had done. Before it went onto the rickety grill a little surprise was inserted into the ground ball of *masa* before it was flattened onto the griddle.

I had tasted one before, but I politely smiled and watched carefully. The thick handmade pupusa was about 31/2 inches in diameter and always stuffed with some surprise. Today the surprise inside would be refried beans. In fact, in this town it was always refried beans if anything at all. Señor Lopez explained the city folks filled their *pupusas* with cheese, sometimes pork. And sometimes not at all. They even had special pupuserias where you could buy them to go.

The old man they called *Abuelo* which meant grandpa showed me the fishing nets they were repairing and the coffee tree that grew coffee beans. We sat on a bench under a tree in the shade of the hot noon sun.

A couple came up to my parents and began to talk to them in Nahuat. It was the indigenous language of El Salvador. Mario's father translated it into English for my parents. "We are poor. Sometimes the soldiers come and kick us off the land and we must move again because this land does not belong to us. We have a child. We want this child to go to school one day. We want this child to have food every day. Please take our child. We know you can provide a better life for her." My parents talked to each other about this and decided they could not take this responsibility. Their lives would be disrupted in ways they could not imagine. I wanted a new little sister like Margarita. But, this was not to be.

I quietly thought to myself. *'I know those shoes were not a big enough trade for a little sister, or brother but shouldn't we get something in return for all the gifts we brought them?'* Elaine saw the look on my face and said "Karen, sometimes it is better to give than to receive."

Señor Lopez quickly changed the subject. He started bargaining for a hammock made from local rope. He did not need one, but he wanted the villagers to be proud of their handiwork. My father watched, and then began to barter for a hammock too. In exchange they traded the shoes we had bought the day before. He explained to them that we had accidentally bought too many. Everyone parted with their hearts and pride still intact that day.

This changed me. After that the *pupusas* I ate at dinner were more about the sharing. Now I knew others who only had beans inside their *pupusa*, while I had cheese and pork. I felt like a *pupusa* newly stuffed with compassion. Someday, I hoped, that memory would reach out to me and surprise others with a kindness when I took a bite out of this moment visiting these kind families.

As we drove away Señor Lopez explained "That was the village where Margarita was born." Mario's little sister was adopted. My mother explained that Margarita's first parents were too poor to buy enough food for her. That was sad, but she always seemed so happy. She was so much fun. I now had a new appreciation for every bite of food I had, the safety of a warm roof over my head, the calmness of my home not worrying about soldiers coming to kick me off the place I lived. Now I understood why Margarita slept with her eyes open. Maybe down deep she was still afraid. Now I know what Señor Lopez meant by the 'biggest present of his life.' It was Margarita! She was a gift. Tomorrow was Christmas Eve. I wondered what gifts were instore for me.

10
LA POSADA
DECEMBER 24

It had been twelve hours since we arrived at the Lopez city home. Tonight, at midnight would be when Christmas eve turned into Christmas Day. Fireworks were prepared. Food was being chopped, diced, fried, and baked in the kitchen. Masa was being ground. The big pot of hot chocolate was being blended with chocolate, sugar, and spices. The fiesta was going to start just hours from now. Midnight was when the Lopez celebrated the birth of Jesus. So, I got to stay up till then. My father explained that here it was more about the "presence" of Jesus, than the "presents" of the three Kings. They told me that Santa had handed over a few presents to the three kings, and maybe he left a few gifts with Grandma.

No one seemed to care about our Ohio traditions. Everyone was in a rush today. There was not even enough time for anyone to chop up bananas for me at breakfast. There was juice and pastries on the table. Señora Lopez was busy preparing for the big party. "There are going to be many guests tonight," Señora Lopez told us. "Who is coming to the party?" I asked. "There will be people dressed as Mary and Joseph tonight for Las Posadas. It is to honor the sacred journey to Bethlehem and people coming to the house looking for posada or shelter. Posada means Inn or Lodging. Everyone in the neighborhood will be included. Spreading love in the community was what this holiday is about." Señora

Lopez explained how the posada people go house to house to celebrate the journey of Mary and Joseph..

Soon people began to arrive. First a mariachi band came and played for all the guests. The entire cast of the nativity and dozens more people arrived dressed as animals, shepherds, and people from the scene of the nativity of Christ. Las Posadas was a feast to honor the sacred journey of Mary and Joseph looking for shelter, and it filled this home with much love and joy. Señor and Señora Lopez had opened their home to remember the innkeeper who provided shelter to the baby Jesus.

People in the neighborhood dressed up as different animals from the nativity set, and angels, and everyone from every home in the neighborhood kept knocking until they came to the house of the Lopezes. They were let in. This was to celebrate the wonderful night that Jesus was born.

There were all kinds of foods to eat. There were tamales, champurrados, tamilatos de rajas, enchiladas, arroz *blanco*, and arroz *rojo* and chocolate. I put everything on my plate and tried to like it all, but mostly I kept going back for seconds, thirds, and fourths of hot chocolate.

My sister, Elaine and I played cards with Mario's younger cousin even though we couldn't speak Spanish. Scott played soccer with the Lopez boys in the courtyard. All the kids were laughing and playing loudly. Señor Lopez stood on the balcony above the courtyard and whistled loudly. Everyone looked up. *"Es tiempo para la piñata!"* he shouted. He held a large star shaped piñata with tassels and brilliantly colored tissue paper. There were diamond shaped sequins on the sides that glistened. Señor Lopez dangled the piñata from the balcony. Then he pointed to Señor Roberto to draw a line on the cement. Señor Roberto then directed all the children to stand behind it. He lined the children up from smallest to largest. He had a baseball bat in his hand and gave it to the smallest little girl, Chiquita Margarita. Chiquita swung, and Señor Lopez dangled the piñata in front of her, so she would just be able to knock the tassel. It almost looked too pretty to bash. I could see why he wanted it to last. It was filled with nuts, candies and goodies for the kids below and was the most colorful shiny toy I had ever seen. Suddenly, I was next. I did not know what was going to happen. This was my first piñata. I just did what Chiquita Margarita did.

I was a bit timid. When I was given the bat, I lightly swung, and swung and missed hitting it after stepping up to the line. The older children were scheming the best angle to get the most candy, so that when it was broken, they could all scramble to the floor and crawl around in the most advantageous way to grab the most candy. Señor Lopez dangled it from the balcony above the courtyard for every child's turn, laughing in delight at their futile efforts. As soon as the older boys would swing, he would pull it away quickly to make it fair for us younger ones. Everyone had completed their two chances to swing. It was Chiquita's third turn. Señor Lopez was able to dangle it just right so that, when it was her turn, it broke. Chiquita bent down and started picking up candy and putting it in her dress pockets. All the big kids pushed and shoved and ran and grabbed candy as fast as they could. I tried to do the same, but by the time I figured out what to do, I only had two handfuls of candy in my pockets.

I was confused and tired because it was getting late. I went to the table and spread out my ten pieces of candy. The older girls came and sat around me and spread their hordes of candy out too and shared their huge piles with me. I went from being sad and confused to feeling part of the fun and warmly included.

After all the posada people left to go to the next house, it was time for the fireworks. My brother Scott was given ten bottle rockets. Elaine, who was four years older than me, had smoke bombs, snakes and fire cracker sticks that made a large pop pop. I was given as many sparklers as I wanted. Outside it was not cold like Ohio in winter, so everyone was out on the street with their fireworks that spun and whirled, and screeched, and made beautiful colors, shapes and sizes in the sky.

I was getting tired and almost forgot it was Christmas Eve. My tummy was heavy from too many cups of hot chocolate. Tired and worried that Santa would never find the Perry family here in the mix of all this, I sat in a daze on the sofa. Señor Lopez kneeled beside me to explain that Santa works with the three wise men here in El Salvador. Santa will give your presents to the wise men and they will leave your presents under your bed or in your shoes when they come to visit the baby Jesus. This seemed to make perfect sense. After all, I couldn't imagine how long it would take Santa to get through customs with all those packages. So, I just got up and went to look at the nativity scene in the formal room of the house.

I saw the ceramic Mary, Joseph, cows, sheep, sitting on the straw. The

Angel Gabriel was flying overhead. The stable was there. The manger was there, but there was no Jesus. Tears welled up in my eyes. Since there was no baby Jesus here, maybe the wise men would not come with their presents. I did not want anyone to know that I was upset. I ran to my mother and began to cry in her lap. This was all so confusing to me.

My mother gently asked, "Why are you crying?" I didn't want to tell my mother. I didn't even know myself if I was upset because of the presents or just was confused about how we were going to do Christmas. I didn't want to sound selfish about presents. After all, the Lopez family had so nicely treated me. I couldn't complain. I got to light more sparklers than I ever had in my whole life. I got to swing at my first piñata. I got to drink as much hot chocolate as I wanted, and nobody made me eat everything on my plate. It was all so overwhelming. I did not know what to say. So instead, just said, "Where is baby Jesus?" Señora Lopez smiled at my mother and said, "Kareñita, they want you to be the Madrina this year. You are the youngest guest here, and Chiquita Margarita has agreed that you should be the Madrina even though she is the youngest child here." I sniffled up my tears and said, "What is that?"

She motioned for my mom and me to come over to the other room. My mother held my hand and we walked into Señora Lopez's bedroom and sat on her neatly made bed. She reached up and pulled down a box. In the box she lifted the tissue paper surrounding the baby Jesus.

"You will get to be the Madrina. That is the most important job of all, because without the Madrina, they cannot have Christmas. The Madrina puts the baby Jesus in the manger at midnight. Only then can they celebrate the birth of Jesus and exchange presents and cards. Can you help us with this?"

I sniffled again, blew my nose in a tissue my mother gave me and pulled my shoulders back. I gulped all my tears away and smiled warmly. A warm feeling glowed in my heart when I held the baby Jesus in my hand. I felt so special inside. I felt the Light of Christ shine in my hands that night. When the clock struck twelve, I gently placed the baby Jesus in the manger. Everyone clapped and hugged and kissed me. I could only imagine how Mary must have felt when she held Jesus for the first time.

That night everyone exchanged presents right after I gently laid Jesus in the manger. The next morning, I found delicately wrapped boxes under my bed from the three wisemen. I don't remember what was in the boxes from the Magi because the biggest gift of all that Christmas was the beautiful moment when I got to be the Madrina.

GLOSSARY OF SPANISH WORDS

Abuela	grandmother
Abuelo	grandfather
al Gusto	to taste
Angelita	little angel
Aqui	here
Arepas	fat corn tortilla
Artes	arts
Asado	pickled
Avenida	Street/avenue
Ayer	yesterday
ayote	squash
avion	airplane
Baile	dance
Bellas	the beautiful

Bosque	*woods*
Chilaquiles	*dish of fried tortilla strips typically topped with a spicy tomato sauce and cheese.*
Chapultepec	*grasshopper*
Claro	*clearly (for sure)*
comida	*food*
con permiso	*excuse me (with your permission)*
cooperativo	*car share*
cuando	*when*
cuando ella viene	*when she comes*
comer	*to eat*
con	*with*
crema	*cream*
cuando	*when*
cuarto	*room*

cuatro	*four*
Cucharra	*spoon*
Come/ comer	*eat/to eat*
con	*with*
crema	*cream*
de	*of*
del	*of the*
desayuno	*breakfast*
diez	*ten*
Diez pesos	*ten pesos*
Dulce	*sweet*
Ella	*she*
El	*the*
Enchiladas	*a rolled tortilla with a filling*
en	*in*
Es	*it is*

Es un	it is a
Folkórico	folk
Faro	fire
Fue	was
grande	big
hija	daughter
Huevos	eggs
la	the
Leche	milk
limón	lemon
lo	it
los	the (plural)
Madrina	godmother, an honorary person to put
	The baby Jesus in the manger
Mi	my
Muertos	the dead

Nueve	*nine*
No es	*It is not*
Nopal	*an edible cactus*
Nosotros	*we*
pajaro	*bird*
Palacio de	*palace of*
para la	*for the*
piñata	*a decorated figure of an animal containing toys and candy*
Platanos	*bananas*
Pimiento	*pepper*
Por supuesto	*of course*
Pupusas	*a popular El Salvadoran, Guatamalen, and Honduran dish made of a thick, corn tortilla filled with anything from meats to cheeses to refried beans to pork rinds.*

Pupuserías	*place that sells pupusas*
Superhombre	*superman*
te caliente	*hot tea*
te	*your*
Tiempo	*time*
Un	*a*
vale la pena	*worth the pain*
Verdes	*green ones*
Que	*that*
Cena	*light evening meal*
Sarape	*a shawl or blanket worn as a cloak in Latin America*
Pacifico	*Pacific*
Posada	*a ritual re-enactment of Mary and Joseph's search for a lodging in Bethlehem, performed just before Christmas.* *plural noun:* **Las Posadas**

Picante	*peppery hot*
Por favor	*please*
quiero	*I want*
platanos	*bananas*
mañana	*morning*
nuestro	*our*
pondrá	*will put*
reciete	*receipt*
Cuanto	*how much*
Cuesta/costar	*cost*
regalo	*gift*
Sabe/saber	*know-to know*
Savina Rojo	*type of very hot red pepper*
Señor	*Mr.*
Señora	*Mrs.*
Sopresa	*surprise*

su	*your*
Tenemos	*we have*
Té	*tea*
Te	*you (direct object)*
totopos	*crisp tortilla triangles, called*
viene/venir	*to come*
Vihuelistas	*a person who plays an old fashioned plucked stringed instrument of Spain, related to the guitar.*
Y	*and*
Yo	*I*

ABOUT THE AUTHOR

Karen White Porter is the Director of Loga Springs Academy and a Nationally Board Certified Teacher. Her Master's Degree in language education gave her a chance to see the importance of emotional intelligence among her students. Teaching around the world shed light on the importance of emotions, culture, and language in learning. She has taught at East China Normal University in Shanghai, China, Hofstra University NY, Hillside Public Schools NJ, Saint Andrews University, Scotland, Belcher Elementary FL, The University of South Florida, The State University of Florida, and Loga Springs Academy. She now builds her own curriculum that builds emotional intelligence. She was inspired by her students as they went on this educational journey with her. After working for over 25 years helping young people identify their feelings and learning passions, she decided she wanted to provide tools to build emotional intelligence to a wider audience. If you would like to schedule a school reading or author presentation please contact her at 352-514-8701.